ABOVE SUSPICION

ABOVE SUSPICION

THE TRUE STORY OF SERIAL KILLER RUSSELL WILLIAMS

ALAN R. WARREN

COPYRIGHT

ABOVE SUSPICION: The True Story of Serial Killer Russell Williams
Written by Alan R. Warren

Published in Canada

Copyright @ 2020 by Alan R. Warren

All rights reserved. No part of this book may be reproduced, scanned, or distributed in any printed or electronic form without permission of the author. The unauthorized reproduction of a copyrighted work is illegal. Criminal copyright infringement, including infringement without monetary gain, is investigated by the FBI and is punishable by fines and federal imprisonment. Please do not participate in or encourage privacy of copyrighted materials in violation of the author's rights. Purchase only authorized editions.

This is a work of nonfiction. No names have been changed, no characters invented, no events fabricated.

Cover design, formatting, layout, and editing by Evening Sky Publishing Services

PREFACE

"In the beginning, it was all black and white." –
Maureen O'Hara

This is the true story of Russell Williams; once the model of a military man, now he sits convicted of a series of crimes that include two counts of first degree murder, brutal sexual assaults and eighty-two home invasions that include a series of strange thefts.

Colonel Russell Williams once seemed the embodiment of the military ideals of duty and honor, pilot for the Prime Minister and Queen Elizabeth of England, commander of the secret Canadian Air Force base in the Persian Gulf, and in 2009 appointed commanding officer of Canada's largest, most important Air Force base in Trenton, Ontario.

Russell Williams's fall from grace is a frightening reminder of the unpredictability of human behavior.

1

TO BE YOUNG AGAIN

"It takes a long time to become young." - Pablo Picasso

Russell Williams

David Russell Williams was born in Bromsgrove, Worcestershire, England on March 7, 1963, to Christine Nonie Chivers and Cedric David Williams. His father received his Ph.D. in Metallurgy (a material scientist who specializes in metals), and was from a privileged family, son of a British civil defense officer. His mother was from a well-to-do family where her father was an executive with British Petroleum Oil.

His family immigrated to Canada, where they moved to Chalk River, Ontario. There his father was hired as a metallurgist at Canada's premiere nuclear research facility, Chalk River Laboratories. It was once a top-secret installation created to help the United States with the Manhattan Project, a research and development project during World War II that produced the first nuclear weapons.

This was also a great place to raise two boys, being only a short distance from Camp Petawawa, where they would be entranced with the constant military flyovers. This was probably where Russell caught the flying bug, by looking up at the incredible aircraft that would fly over.

After relocating to Chalk River, the Williams family met another family, the Sovkas, Jerry and Marilynn, who moved only about one block away from them. Both being new to town, they soon they became close friends. Jerry was a nuclear physicist from Alberta and a son of Czechoslovakian immigrants. Marilynn was born in Glasgow, Scotland, a daughter of a doctor. The two families would end up spending a lot of time together. They would hire one babysitter, who would take care of both families' children in one of their homes, while the parents spent time together in the other home.

The town was considered quite a conservative town, but there was a small group of people that were involved in a "swingers club" where they would be involved in swapping out each other's wives. We do not know if the Williamses and Sovkas were involved in this group, but it comes into question later when they ended up divorcing and remarrying each other's spouse.

It was not long after they were settled in the new life that Christine, Russell's mother, opened her own private physiotherapy practice, specializing in children's needs. This was not a popular thing to do in the community. In those days it was not thought of too well, that a wife of a prominent Ph.D. would work outside of her home; a good wife would stay at home with the family. This business would also be considered a challenge to her husband as the breadwinner of the family.

Perhaps this was the start of their drifting apart in their relationship. By the time Russell turned six, his mother packed up the two boys and moved to their own residence. The break-up was smooth at the beginning, with both parents settling on a visitation schedule and finances. But soon after that, it turned for the worse; Christine found out that David was having an affair with Marilynn Sovka. This was a betrayal as Marilynn had been such a close friend. The rumors spread in the small town quickly, as there weren't many places to hide such a thing. Christine filed for divorce soon afterwards.

This divorce was the reason for an evaluation on Russell, the first that we have on record. The following is a copy of the report.

"David Russell, born on March 7, 1963, in Cardiff, England, is in good health and appears to be an active, precocious child with an interest in life and people. He appeared to have a close relationship with the petitioner (mother) who is very involved in

> her children's activities. Russell appears very compatible with his brother. He is attending grade one in the Herman Street Public School, Petawawa, and appears above average in reading and printing ability. His creative ability appears mature and vocabulary expansive. Russell's relationship with the respondent (father) is also very close and he enjoys visits with him."

Exactly one week after the Williamses dissolved their marriage, the Sovkas had officially ended their marriage as well. Now while all of this was happening, the former Mrs. Williams and Mr. Sovka had somehow fallen in love. They not only ended up moving in with each other, they were married only four months later. It was such a scandal in the community that they felt forced to move away, to North York, a suburb of Toronto. This way they could start fresh where nobody would know of their past. This was also when Russell and his brother took their new stepfather's last name, to become Sovkas.

Meanwhile, his father, David, tried staying in town with Marilynn as his new girlfriend, but they could only last a year before they felt compelled to move as well. They found the tension mounting and thought moving away would relieve that. So they headed to North York, but that didn't help, and they found themselves separating within a year of their move.

Russell then began high school at Toronto's Birchmount Park Collegiate and started to deliver *The Globe and Mail* newspaper for work. His mother had him taking piano lessons, and he joined the school band where he played the trumpet. It was there that Russell met his first girlfriend, Sara, who was a flute player in the school band. Sara was known as a happy girl who liked to play jokes on others. They were inseparable for the two years that they dated. Nobody knows the reasons they broke up or how Russell handled it.

By 1979, Russell's family was on the move again. This time they moved to South Korea where Jerry, his stepfather, was to oversee another reactor project. Neither of the boys seemed to settle very well in their new home or with the new culture. In fact, Russell was apparently disturbed by the way that women were treated in South Korea. He would find himself getting into fights with the Korean men, as they liked to spit on the women that they were angry with.

After only one year, Russell was sent back to Toronto, and he completed his final two years of high school as a boarding student at Toronto's Upper Canada College, while his parents stayed in South Korea.

One of his roommates at college ended up becoming a lifelong friend, Jeff Farquhar. Jeff claimed,

> "Russell was known as a real prankster among the dorm. He would do things like pull plastic wrap over their toilet bowls, or pour soy sauce in somebody's unattended drink. He seemed to have a passion for catching his roommates off guard, by hiding in the closet, and jumping out to scare them."

Soon the life of every woman on campus was about to change in a much more terrifying way than any of the pranks Russell liked to play on any of them. In May of 1987, a series of brutal attacks and rapes began on campus by someone who was soon to become known as "The Scarborough Rapist." In many of the cases reported, women were followed getting off their school bus and assaulted quite viciously in nearby parks or parking lots.

Several years later, Paul Bernardo was linked by DNA to many of the rapes that were committed during the years of 1987-1990. Bernardo has since been convicted and now serves life in Kingston Penitentiary for many of the rapes. However, despite his confessions of many attacks, there are still quite a few cases that remain unsolved, and Bernardo has denied involvement in them.

Strangely enough, both Bernardo and Williams attended the same Economics Program and, in fact, Bernardo finished only one year behind him. There was a report in the *Toronto Sun* newspaper that suggested Paul Bernardo and Williams not only went to the same classes, but also were friends and hung out together. But Russell's best friend, Jeff Farquhar, has since denied that saying,

---

"If Russell had known Bernardo, I would have too!"

After studying Economics for four years, Russell had suddenly announced that he wanted to join the Air Force and told his friend Farquhar, "I think I want to be a pilot!" This left Farquhar in shock. He told CBC,

> "Where did that come from? I was a little bit concerned because he was taking it way over the top. I really thought he was trying to live like Tom Cruise in Top Gun; so did a lot of us. I knew Russ well, and I thought he's really lost in a fantasy world here, and I kept thinking to myself, oh no, now he's going to be a jet fighter?"

In years to come, Russell would make his fantasy a reality becoming one of Canada's top pilots, flying not only fighter jets, but transport planes to war zones and natural disasters and carrying the Prime Minister and the Queen of England across the country and around the World.

Through it all, Russell remained friends with Farquhar after college, and even was the emcee at his wedding. But there were some things Russell didn't share with his friend, like his impending marriage. "It was a complete shock to me," Farquhar said. "I mean, I was excited for him, but he hadn't been dating from University days, say, from second year on."

On June 1, 1991, Russell married Mary Elizabeth Harriman, who was the Associate Director of the Heart and Stroke Foundation of Canada.

Mary Elizabeth Harriman

Mary Elizabeth Harriman was born on November 15, 1957, the only daughter of Frederick and Irene Harriman. She also had a brother named Peter who died as an infant. Harriman's father, Frederick, was a decorated military veteran who had spent five years overseas during the Second World War. He came back to study geology at the University of New Brunswick and later worked in mining exploration in Newfoundland, Quebec and Northern Ontario.

Her mother, Irene Lavigne, had been a stenographer at a mining company in Rouyn-Noranda, Quebec. Mary Elizabeth grew up in Madsen, Ontario, which was a rough mining town.

Mary was a student at the Red Lake District High School where she graduated with honors. Harriman went to the University of Guelph, Ontario, and graduated with a Bachelor of Science degree in 1980. She later attended the University of St. Francis Xavier to get her Master's in Education.

It was sometime in the late 1980s when Mary must have been introduced to Russell Williams. Harriman was five years older than Russell, but the two seemed to get along well.

The couple moved to Orleans, Ontario, which is a suburb of Ottawa, the Capitol of Canada. Williams had now been posted as Directorate of Air Requirements at the National Defense Headquarters. He served at the Airlift Capability Projects Strategic and Tactical, and Fixed-Wing Search and Rescue. In 1994, he was then posted to the 412 Transport Squadron in Ottawa, where he transported VIPs, including high-ranking government officials and foreign dignitaries. Williams was promoted to Major in 1999 and posted to Director General Military Careers in Ottawa, where he served as the multi-engine pilot career manager.

Williams obtained his Master of Defense Studies from the Royal Military College of Canada in 2004 with a 55-page thesis that supported preemptive war in Iraq and, in July of 2004, was promoted to Lieutenant Colonel. From there he was moved to Camp Mirage, a secretive logistics facility believed to be located at Al Mirage Air Force Base in Dubai, United Arab Emirates, that provides support to Canadian Forces operations in Afghanistan, where he served as commanding officer for seven months.

The commanding officer of Canada's Air Force was then Lieutenant-General Angus Watt. Now retired, the General says that

> "even under the constant scrutiny and evaluation of military life, Williams was one of the best and brightest, usually calm, very logical, very rational and able to produce good quality staff work in a fairly short time which is a valued commodity in Ottawa."

He was promoted to Colonel by the recommendation of the now-retired Lieutenant-General Angus Watt.

On July 15, 2009, Williams was sworn in as the Wing Commander at the Canadian Air Force Base Trenton by the outgoing Wing Commander, Brigadier General Mike Hood. CAFB Trenton is Canada's busiest air transport base and the focus of support for the overseas military operations. Located in Trenton, Ontario, the base also functions as the point of arrival for the bodies of all Canadian Air Force personnel killed in Afghanistan and the starting point for funeral processions along the "Highway of Heroes" when their bodies are brought in for autopsies in Toronto.

Williams had flown Queen Elizabeth II and the Duke of Edinburgh, the Governor General of Canada, the Prime Minister of Canada, and many other dignitaries across Canada and overseas in Canadian Air Force VIP aircraft.

| Williams and Mary

2

WELCOME TO OUR TOWN

"We live in a world that has narrowed into a neighborhood before it has broadened into a brotherhood." – Lyndon B. Johnson

---

Russell Williams and his wife had bought a cottage located in Tweed, Ontario. This was to save Russell from driving back and forth from their Ottawa home to Trenton Air Force Base five days a week.

On a weekend in the Fall 2007, a series of unusual break-ins began to unfold in and around Tweed. Russell Williams was at his cottage and neighbor Larry Jones was at home next door when he got frantic phone call from his daughter who lived nearby. She'd come home from a party, surprised an intruder in jogging clothes.

"Christine opened the door to go from the garage

> into the house and saw this long, tall figure run past the door on the deck. He jumped over the fence and run off in the bush,"

---

she told Jones. She thought it was just one of the neighborhood kids and nothing seemed to be missing. It would be years before the police told her something different. In fact, it would be years before anyone put it together that beginning in 2007, per court documents, when Russell Williams was at his cottage in Tweed, a multitude of bizarre break-ins would follow with women's lingerie and underwear stolen, almost all in his own neighborhood, especially on Cosy Cove Lane.

It was the same pattern as the break-ins in the nearby Ottawa suburb of Orleans, that sometimes were so well executed they weren't even noticed. We can't possibly know exactly what went on in each of the homes that Williams broke into, or what caused him to commit these bizarre crimes. Some believe it was the drugs, like Prednisone, that he was taking to relieve the pain that he suffered from arthritis.

There are several of the invasions that he decided to record with photos or by camcorder and keep for himself, eventually found by the police, that tell us some things that he did during his invasions into other people's homes.

On the night of Saturday, September 8, 2007, Ron and Monique Murdoch, Williams's next door neighbors on Cosy Cove Lane, had to leave town with their two children to visit her gravely ill mother in Sudbury, Ontario, about a six-hour drive from their home.

Williams had gotten to know the Murdoch family very

well over the past few years. Quite often he had been invited over for dinner and played cards with them until late. Their daughter, Samantha, who was twelve years old at the time, even showed Williams how to play crib and baked muffins for him. What made him decide to choose their house, we will probably never know. Knowing that his neighbors had gone for at least a couple of nights, the Colonel, I guess, just couldn't resist the empty house.

About 9:30 p.m., he crept across the dark yard and let himself in an unlocked rear door. He headed straight for their daughter Samantha's bedroom, where he started taking photos with his camera. The pictures started out with broad, general pictures of the whole room, but it soon narrowed in on her dresser drawers. More specifically, her underwear drawers. Soon after that, he moved to her closet and took pictures of her clothes that were hanging, and then of her bed.

Sometime soon after he finished taking that series of pictures, he removed all his clothes. He then put on a pair of Samantha's pink panties and posed for some portraits, focusing on his protruding penis. He continued taking more pictures, like a photo shoot. He would pose in front of her mirror, hanging her pink panties from his erect penis. He then moved to her bed, where he lay naked with his legs spread and started to masturbate. He took plenty of time to set up his tripod, adjusting different angles to get shots that he must have found exciting. He then tried on more of the girl's panties, and even her training bras. He is thought to have spent about three hours there that night and had taken several photos that clearly showed his ejaculation all over Samantha's underwear and bras.

14 | ABOVE SUSPICION

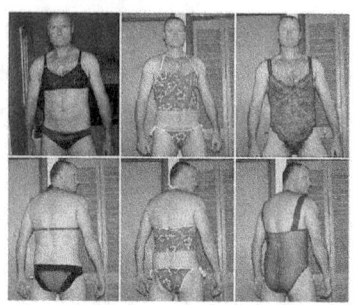

Russell's Selfies

When the Murdochs returned from their trip, they noticed nothing out of the ordinary, and certainly had no reason to; after all, they had the most trusted man in the community taking care of their house. The crime remained unknown for some time. It was three weeks later that Monique's mother passed away. The funeral was planned for Saturday, September 29, 2007, so the family was off again to Sudbury, Ontario.

Williams would take the opportunity to break into their house again. He entered through the same back door, only it was about 11:30 p.m. He went directly to the girl's room again. He was much quicker this time, as he knew what he wanted to do. He removed all his clothes, set up his camera, and this time grabbed her panties and other garments from the dirty laundry basket. Already erect by this time, he started to pose in front of the bedroom mirror, this time not only wearing different pairs of panties, but also tried on her skirts and bras. It didn't take long for him to get erect, so while removing each garment, he would hang it over his penis and take another picture. Again, he would masturbate and leave his ejaculate onto her panties and take pictures of that as well.

Again, when the Murdochs returned, they noticed nothing out of the ordinary. Williams soon came over to offer his condolences. He acted normal and they felt no awkwardness around him at all.

In October, just a few weeks later, Williams struck again. This time with a different neighbor. Larry Jones's daughter house had twin daughters herself, age 11 at the time. During the evening's festivities, he followed much the same pattern. He took several photos of the girls' room, the mother's room, and their underwear drawers, and even clothes that were inside the dryer. Williams stole a total of 23 pairs of underwear from all three females. Later, pictures were found of the girls' underpants spread out across his cottage floor in different types of display, almost like a catalogue.

In total, Williams had done this same type of procedure eighty-two times, in forty-eight different homes; thirteen of the targets were females under the age of eighteen. It must be said that most of these break-ins remained unknown at the time; in fact, only one report of a break-in was reported in Tweed, and fifteen in Orleans, out of forty-eight homes that were broken into.

It took one more year, in June of 2008, when he started to elevate the items that he would take from the houses. In this case, he stole a sex toy that belonged to the 24-year-old resident, as well as her undergarments.

In October of 2008, he upped his risk level even more. Until now, he seemed to have been proud of the fact that he had done so many break-ins, which the victims had not even realized, and had not been discovered. But this time it would be different. Williams broke into a house in Ottawa where a family with three girls lived. In one of the girls' rooms, he had taken her photo album out, opened it to a page of her own pictures, and left it on her bed. In another girl's room, he scattered a bunch of her 4x6 pictures of herself across her bedroom floor, and in the 12-year old girl's room, he logged into her computer, looked through her private pictures, and left a message: "Merci."

Williams continued to up the stakes of his crimes. Later that year he broke into a house of a family that had a fifteen-year old girl. He headed straight to her room, as he did on his other invasions, but this time he found a pair of her panties that had a bloodstain on them. This apparently aroused him so much that he took pictures of himself licking the stain on the panties, as well as wearing them over his face like a mask, and finally masturbating on the stain. In all, he took over seventy pictures of that visit. While the girl later realized that several of her panties were missing, the parent did not report it to the police, thinking it was just a prank being played on her by her step-siblings.

On January 1, 2009, New Year's Day, Brenda Constantine, her husband Brian Rogers, and their 15-year-old daughter were away to Toronto, when Williams made his first break-in to their home. He took several photos of the girl's bedroom, removed all the underwear from her drawers and took them home with him. He was rather quick, far less than an hour, not his usual visit. He returned the next night, but this time he must have been far more comfortable, as he stripped down naked as soon as he arrived. He then followed his normal ritual by taking photos of himself both naked and dressed in the girl's clothing.

In one of the photos, he took the girl's make-up brush

and brushed it along his erect penis several times. He then put the brush back for her to use again. This night, instead of taking just panties and bras, he also took some dresses, a tank top, and even shoes.

Later in an interview on CBC's *The Fifth Estate*, the family described their ordeal. Soon after they got home from their trip, their teenage girl was unpacking and noticed something strange. Brenda said,

---

"My daughter came running down the stairs telling us that all her underwear was gone out of her drawer! And we kind of laughed and said, 'check the floor' because you know how teenagers are, 'check the laundry' or whatever. She said, 'no, I'm serious, there's nothing left in my drawers.'"

Brenda Constantine and her husband Brian Rogers would start to take their daughter's claims much more seriously when their daughter also discovered what else was missing.

"She went back upstairs to realize there was dresses, shoes, and all of her bathing suits and even photographs of herself gone."

Someone had gone through their family albums selecting pictures of their 15-year-old daughter, and police found something even more disturbing. Brenda said,

> "They did tell us that they took some DNA evidence from my daughter's bedroom from around her bureau, where the underwear drawer was, around that area. They wanted us to wash everything clean, and of course my daughter didn't want to sleep in her bedroom for three months."

This must have been very terrifying for the family as somebody was targeting their 15-year-old girl. Brenda continued,

> "We wouldn't let her go anywhere or do anything alone. She wasn't allowed to stay home alone and her brothers were basically her bodyguards as well as we had friends looking out for her as well."

After speaking to the police, Constantine and Roger learned of some other break-ins that were in the area, that had similar thefts, so they decided to call a town meeting. Even though the heat was on and the police were looking for a serial thief, Williams would continue his series of many more home intrusions. He would keep to the same patterns, only taking more pieces of clothing in each case. In some cases, he would take as many as 168 pieces just from one person.

When Williams took command in Trenton, the demands on Williams increased. He was now responsible for thousands of military men and women and often in the public eye. But following his promotion in July 2009, per police records, the frequency of the break-ins increased, too. There were ten more in his first two months as Wing Commander, and all the while, Colonel Williams performed his official duties.

THE FIRST ASSAULT

It was only a few hours after Williams returned home from his trip to Alaska that he made his first physical assault on a woman. He had selected a young woman whose name remains unknown to the public. He probably spotted her on one of his many jogs around the area, where he always learned about his victims' living arrangements and lifestyles. Not much has been revealed about this assault. Even the victim's name still has not been released, even after she later filed a civil lawsuit against Williams. He spent two hours in which he forced the woman to strip, and he took many photos of her. All during this time, he would stop to touch her privates. Maybe he had to be quick, as the very next morning at 8:30 a.m., he had to meet with the Criminal Intelligence Service of Ontario. Officer Kevin West, who was at the meeting, later told *Maclean's* magazine,

---

"He was the same as he was every day,"

---

and didn't notice any difference in his demeanor.

MURDER OF CORPORAL COMEAU

| Corporal Marie-France Comeau

Corporal Marie-France Comeau was born into a military family in 1972. Her dad was a Canadian Armed Forces medic, and one of her grandfathers had earned honors as a pilot in World War II. Growing up listening to the war stories of both men greatly excited the young girl, who at an early age made an important decision: she would join the Air Force. She ended up among the crew that escorted Prime Minister Stephen Harper to Mumbai in November 2009. Now back from that trip that she had always dreamed about, she was looking forward to telling her boyfriend all about it.

However, while she was away, a predator had been on his own trip, only to her home. One week before, knowing that she was away, Williams had made a reconnaissance trip to her home. He found the rear basement window unlocked. It was large enough for him to fit through. He checked out her bathroom and closets to make sure that there were no signs of a man living there. He also couldn't resist the bedroom, where he would find her sex toys, bras and panties, some of which he couldn't help but to try on, and even take with him to his own home.

It was 11 p.m. and Williams had made the same trip to her house again, entering her home the same way that he had done the week previously. He was now in her basement, waiting for her to go to bed and fall asleep.

Marie-France was on the phone with her boyfriend, setting up dinner plans with him so that she could share all the events of her recent trip. After finishing her call, Marie-France realized she had not seen her cat, Bixby. Starting her search, she headed for the basement, knowing that was his favorite hiding spot. "Bixby, where are you?" she yelled from the top of the stairs. She turned on the basement lights and started down the stairs to find her cat. "There you are." She walked toward the cat, bent down to pick him up, and just then she saw a dark figure behind the furnace and screamed loudly.

Knowing he must silence her right away, he smashed his flashlight over her head. This only made her want to fight, even though she could feel the blood on her head. It took several more blows before she would fall backwards. Williams then lunged on top of her, which smeared her blood across the cement floor. He bound her wrists with rope. He stood her up and pushed her against a metal jack support post where a steel pin ripped into her upper back. He then tied her firmly to the post and covered her mouth with duct tape.

Now that his victim was secured, he would now make sure that they would not be interrupted. He took her house key, which had been left on the kitchen table, and snapped it off in the lock of the front door, so that nobody that had a key could get in. He then headed for her bedroom and ripped the comforter off her bed and covered her bedroom window with it.

He headed back to the basement, not paying attention to the trail of blood that he was leaving with his shoes. He removed the duct tape from her mouth and cut the ties to the post so that he could bring her upstairs to the bedroom. While starting up the stairs, Marie started to scream. He quickly grabbed her head and smashed it against the wall, creating a spray of blood and a head-shaped crater. Marie now dropped to the floor unconscious.

Williams now felt compelled to get his camera and take four pictures of her lying naked and bleeding on the floor, including a close-up of her vagina and the cuts on her breasts and face. Williams then carried her up to her bedroom and placed her onto the bed in a fetal position. He grabbed a towel from the bathroom and wrapped it around her head, covering her eyes and nose, then wrapping it with duct tape to keep it in place. He then set up his camcorder on a tripod at the foot of the bed, focusing on the still-unconscious Marie, pressed record, and started to undress.

He climbed onto the bed wearing nothing except a

black skull cap which covered his face. He forced Marie onto her back and spread her legs and lined her up for penetration. She then moaned as he began to rape her. Not caring about her protest, he grabbed his camera, which he had placed on the bed, and started taking pictures of the penetration. After 17 minutes of raping her in several different positions, only stopping to take random pictures, Williams then removed his face mask, and smiled smugly at the camcorder while rubbing her breasts and stomach.

All the while Marie was telling him to "get out, I want you to leave" but he didn't answer.

Williams then whispered, "Stay there," and again got up from the bed, smiled into the camcorder again, and grabbed and squeezed some KY jelly onto his fingers. He moved back towards the bed and applied the lubricant to her genitals. He climbed back on top of her and, after a few more minutes of intercourse, looked back into the camera, withdrew, and carefully caught his ejaculate into his cupped hand.

Now on his way into the bathroom, she wondered if she could try and escape? Hearing the toilet flush, she slid herself off the bed. She heard Williams walk into the living room, so she headed for the bathroom, and slammed the door closed behind her, hoping to get the door locked behind her before he noticed she was no longer on the bed. But she wasn't fast enough; he smashed through the door and threw her against the bathroom wall. He grabbed her by the hair and dragged her back into the bedroom, pushing her into a seated position on the bed. "Now stay here," he told her boldly. He forced intercourse on her again, followed by another round of photographs.

After he finished, Williams then rifled through her

drawers, took out select pieces of underwear and laid them on her body, and took more pictures. It was like he wanted to model her in different garments and create a catalogue for himself. He then started placing them into his duffel bag, perhaps as souvenirs that he could have for future benefit to relieve himself with.

She then began to moan loudly and move back and forth on the bed. He quickly lay down beside her and said told her to be quiet. "No, please," she replied, "I don't want to die."

"You're not going to die," Williams answered quickly, and the struggle went on like this back and forth for several minutes.

He then placed more duct tape around her face, covering her mouth and nose this time. According to the police transcripts, she then died of suffocation, due to her airways being covered with duct tape.

It was now 4 a.m. and he had to be at an important meeting in Ottawa, about a three-hour drive, so Williams had no time to go home. Before leaving, he threw all the sheets from her bed, and the comforter that he had hung over the window, into the wash and doused them in bleach, only not realizing that he had left his shoe print in the trail of blood, a mistake that would soon catch up to him.

The next morning, November 25, Comeau's boyfriend became worried, as she had not shown up for work, and he had just spoken to her the previous night, very unlike Marie-France. He then went over to her home and let himself in. Outside, Comeau's neighbor, Terry Alexander, had a plumber who had come to his house for repairs.

He recalls Marie-France's boyfriend suddenly bursting out of the home, running across the street, tears running down his face. "Did you see any strange people or cars around here?" he shouted. "She's lying dead inside," he said before breaking down into sobs.

Two days later, investigations concluded that Comeau's death had been a homicide. Investigators from Northumberland OPP (Ontario Provincial Police) spent a few weeks looking for evidence, even stripping the floors down to the concrete and ripping out the cabinets in the kitchen.

The neighbors in the small town were afraid, and rumors began to spread, many having different theories on the events that had taken place. Many neighbors had not known her well. Terry Alexander spoke of her shyness, and another neighbor said that he had never seen her around the block.

Her ex-boyfriend, Alain Plante, who was a basic training instructor, had spent more than four years with her, and his son Etienne had loved the woman like his mother.

The Corporal was buried on December 4, 2009, at the National Military Cemetery in Ottawa. Many family members, fellow military officers, and friends attended the ceremony.

An ironic and perhaps angering fact is that as her commanding officer, Williams was tasked with writing an official letter of condolence to her father. He also attended the funeral and participated, reading a eulogy for Comeau who, until now, nobody could have imagined had been murdered by the Colonel himself.

MURDER OF JESSICA LLOYD

Jessica Lloyd

Jessica Lloyd was a 27-year-old brunette with green eyes who loved to smile. She lived alone in a red brick bungalow on a desolate stretch of rural Highway 37 between Belleville and Tweed. She was really into fitness and would often exercise on her treadmill in her basement with her curtains wide open. Jessica worked at the Tri-Board Student Transportation Services where she was the administrator of a school bus line. Friends and family members described her as outgoing, popular, and close with her loved ones, who she talked to daily.

One morning in late January 2010, Russell was running along the highway when he spotted her. She was exercising on her treadmill in the basement. Williams stopped and pretended to be tying his shoes as he watched her for a while, becoming sexually aroused at the sight of her.

A few nights later, on January 28, while driving by her home, he noticed the absence of her car. He pulled off the rural highway into a vacant lot that was situated beside her home. It was in total darkness, but a clear full moon was out that evening, making it easy to find his way through the field to her home. He found the rear sliding glass patio door unlocked, and he let himself into the house. The interior was dark, but he had his flashlight, so he decided to prowl around carefully, get to know the layout of the house.

As previously with Marie-France Comeau, he made his way through the bathroom and closets to make sure that there were no men living there. Having assured himself that Jessica lived alone, he left the house and made his way back through the field to his vehicle.

Around 9 p.m. that night, he saw a car pull into the driveway. Somebody got out of the driver's side of the car and went to the front door. After a few minutes, whoever it was got back into their car and left.

Then about 10:30 p.m., he saw another car pull into the driveway. He waited to make sure it was Jessica and that she was alone. It wasn't long before she made her way to bed, and the house became dark.

He quietly made his way back into the house through

the same back patio door that he had done earlier. He covered his face with the same black skull cap that he had used before. When he entered her bedroom, he saw her lying still, and he was sure she was already asleep.

Williams moved towards her with his flashlight, ready to strike her unconscious, when Jessica's eyes suddenly opened. "Don't scream," he warned her. "Lie on your tummy," he then ordered. Totally frightened, she froze; she then rolled over, and he tied her hands with rope behind her back. "Keep your eyes shut. You don't want to see me," he said as he pulled her up on her feet.

He led Jessica out into the hallway where he stopped to take some photos. He then wrapped duct tape around her eyes and placed her back on her bed, securing her tied hands to the headboard. He set up his camcorder at the foot of the bed, just as he had done before in Comeau's house, and aimed it at Jessica and started filming. Taking a military grade knife from his duffel bag, he slashed through her thin top, exposing her breasts. He then removed her panties, grabbed the camcorder, and started to film up and down her body.

He then gave her the command, "Spread your legs, bend your knees and open your mouth," and he continued to film. "Now close it,, her reluctance was obvious. "You want to survive this, don't you?" he exclaimed.

"Yes," she said.

"Okay, good," he said reassuringly while he removed his own clothing. He took more close-up pictures and asked her, "Why do you shave your pussy?"

"I don't know, I just do, I have for a while," she answered. He proceeded to pose her in a variety of positions while he continued to take pictures.

Williams then removed two black plastic zip ties from his bag and fastened them around her neck and tightened them. "What do you think is happening now?" he asked.

"I don't know," she replied. While holding the camcorder, he walked towards Jessica and tugged on the black ties.

"You feel that?" She nodded. "If I feel something I don't like, I pull on that, and you die. You got it? Do you want to die?" She shook her head no. "Open your mouth." He then focused the camera on her terrified face. He forced his penis into her mouth, still holding the black ties in his hand. He then forced her to continue the fellatio, pausing only to take pictures. Minutes later, he reached orgasm and forced her to swallow his ejaculate.

A few minutes later, Williams was startled by a noise. He suddenly left the bedroom to go look around for the source of the noise. He then asked her, "Do you have a cat?"

She responded, "No."

Williams returned to the room and quickly dressed. He then helped Jessica get dressed by selecting a pair of jeans, a hoodie and a pair of brown shoes. He had quickly decided to change his plans and take Jessica back to his place.

He then led her across the dark field, as she still had the towel and duct tape wrapped around her face, and placed her into the front passenger seat of his truck and drove the 25 minutes back to his home. It was now 4:30 a.m. He continued doing what he was doing with her earlier. He insisted that she take a shower and helped her get undressed, then put her into the shower. Before he climbed into the shower with her, he set up his camcorder to record the event.

After he finished with her in the shower, he dried her off and led her into his bedroom, placed her on the bed, and tied a rope around both of their wrists, so that she couldn't leave the bed without waking him. After they slept for a few hours, she woke Williams up by convulsing and asking him to take her to the hospital. It seemed to startle Williams. He removed the ropes from her wrist and helped her pull her pants and sweater on. He sat on the bed beside her and started rubbing her head as if to calm her. Jessica asked him,

---

"If I die, will you make sure my mom knows that I love her?"

We don't know what happened next, as the camera was stopped. The next time the camera was started again, Jessica was still fully clothed and sleeping on the floor; her plan to get medical help had failed. Over the next several hours, he then made her wear different pairs of panties and bras while he took pictures of her in different poses that he would suggest.

He then told Jessica that it was time to go, and he would safely drop her back at her home. She walked ahead of him, still blindfolded, into his cold garage. Just before getting into his truck, he smashed her over the head with his flashlight to render her unconscious. Instead she collapsed to the floor as a large pool of blood surrounded her head. She was still breathing, so he took the rope and tied it around her neck and pulled it tightly until her body went limp.

His first impulse was to go get his camera and take pictures of the freshly killed woman. Shortly after he took the pictures, he had to get dressed and ready to go to work as he was scheduled for 5:30 a.m. He would dispose of the body later. He then placed the corpse in his garage before dumping it on a road a short distance from his cottage, taking note of the exact location. A few hours later, he piloted a troop flight to California.

On the morning of Friday, January 29, fellow employees realized that Lloyd had not showed up at work and notified her family. Andy Lloyd, her brother who lived in Belleville, and their mother, Roxanne McGarvey, were immediately alarmed by this, and knew something bad must have happened. "It drew a red flag so quick," Andy said. "It just wasn't like her." The two rushed to her house to see what had happened.

On arrival, they found her purse, wallet, and glasses inside, along with her identification. Her car remained in the driveway, but Lloyd herself was missing.

One person who helped in the search noticed footprints outside her bedroom window, footprints that didn't belong to Lloyd.

The Belleville police were notified of her disappearance within 24 hours, and ground and aerial searches began to unfold over the weekend. They were joined by neighboring Stirling-Rawdon police department and the CFB Trenton military base.

Cops and over 150 civilians volunteered to collect information from neighboring residences.

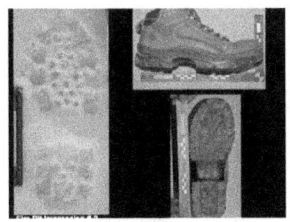

The Lloyds family, friends, and hundreds of people from nearby communities met at the local Tim Horton's coffee shop to hand out missing person posters, which they hoped would help solve the case.

The days went by, to no avail.

Warnings were sent out to nearby residents, telling them to be vigilant. Women who lived alone were urged to change their routines and secure their homes. Local media in Ottawa began to report on the case, and social media became involved with friends organizing groups on Facebook to share any updates on the case. As time passed by, the family lost hope.

Meanwhile, Williams's life resumed, the professional Colonel once again taking over. He would soon be searching for another woman who would lose her life after a humiliating ordeal.

FUNERAL FOR JESSICA

It was just under a week, after Williams's arrest, that the funeral for Jessica Lloyd was held. Just over 300 people gathered to pay their final respects. Reverend Cathy Paul led the hour-long service, and there were several eulogies from close friends and relatives. John, who was Jessica's cousin, spoke for the family as her brothers and sisters were too emotional to speak.

John recalled Jessica's love for the Toronto Maple

Leafs hockey team. "But I think God's going to have a problem with that one," he exclaimed, hoping to lighten the somber room. "Jess was very proud of her heritage, and she is very proud of the men and women in uniform." He slowly lost control and the tears started rolling down his face. "They are strong for us every day, so at this time, I ask for friends, our family, and the whole region of Quinte to be strong for them." He then thanked everyone for all the support they had offered.

Ontario Provincial Police, Belleville police, military police and local politicians all joined together to form an honor guard beside the funeral home as the Lloyd family left the building. Among those that were there were the mayor of Belleville, the acting commander of CFB Trenton, Lieutenant-Colonel David Murphy, and the police chief of Belleville Police Department. As the procession ended, bagpipers played "Amazing Grace."

5

INTERVIEW WITH RUSSELL WILLIAMS

"You didn't have the advantage of being able to interview the victim." – Danny Pino

After 27-year-old Jessica Lloyd went missing on January 28, 2010, the police had received tips from three motorists, all recalling a vehicle parked in the field by Jessica's house on the night of her disappearance. Investigators soon narrowed down the possible vehicles that could have left those tire track impressions.

Police then analyzed the footwear impressions that were left by the tire tracks in the field and in Jessica's backyard. The tread pattern for the smaller set of prints were a match for Jessica's brown suede shoes. Based on these discoveries, police decided to set up a road block to look for any vehicles that matched the specific tires that had been identified.

On Thursday, February 4, exactly one week after Lloyd

had disappeared, the Ontario Provincial Police set up a road block on Highway 37. They hoped to find something to do with the case, perhaps even come across their yet unknown suspect. They canvassed all the motorists using the highway near the missing woman's home from 7 p.m. to 6 a.m., paying attention to tire treads, one of the very few pieces of evidence that they had of the possible suspect.

Williams normally drove this route from work every day, only instead of driving his usual BMW, he had been driving his Pathfinder, the same vehicle he had used to commit the crime. The officer that stopped Williams was initially impressed, with him being a Colonel and commander of the Air Force base in Trenton. He collected Williams's information and asked him if he knew Jessica Lloyd. Williams replied,

---

"I don't know Miss Lloyd and haven't seen anything unusual on my drives by her house."

The officer then with a short wave said, "Thank you, sir, good night," and sent Williams on his way home. But as he drove away, the officer's partner noticed that the tires were a match for what they were looking for.

Of course, the match by itself wasn't enough to stop him at the time, just a lead that they would make a report on. Williams probably drove away quite relieved, believing that he had gotten away with his crimes again. Little did he know that he was now under police surveillance.

As investigators thought more about Williams and the proximity of the Colonel's residence to all the sexual assaults, as well as being Marie-Frances's commanding officer and the tire match, it was time to bring Williams in for an interview.

On Sunday, February 7, just before 2 p.m., Williams received a call at his Ottawa residence by officer Sergeant Jim Smyth of the OPP, requesting that he come in for questioning. Williams simply accepted and went to Ottawa Police Headquarters that day, not even requesting a lawyer. We still don't know why he would have gone to police headquarters to be interviewed without any counsel. Perhaps being a military officer, he was not afraid to go head to head with a police detective. Maybe he thought that the interrogation would be a simple, harmless procedure done on all the motorists that were stopped at the road block. Perhaps he thought that he could just talk himself out of any trouble if it arose. However, what followed would be the turning point in the case, in which Colonel Russell Williams was finally caught.

On February 7, 2010, Williams was interrogated at Ottawa Police Service headquarters by Detective Staff Sergeant Jim Smyth. The interview started at 3 p.m. and by 7:45 p.m., he was describing his crimes. The interrogation lasted approximately ten hours.

Williams entered the room with a lot of confidence, even chewing gum, seeming quite relaxed. He threw his jacket over the back of the chair and took a seat. Then he threw his gloves onto the desktop that was in front of him.

"I'm going to move your gloves," said Detective Smyth. "As you can see here, everything is being videotaped and audiotaped."

"Check," Williams arrogantly responded.

"Ever been interviewed by the police in a room like this before?" Smyth asked. Williams then smiled and looked up at the camera that was mounted on the ceiling.

"I have never been interviewed by the police," he said and grinned, "I guess the closest, I was interviewed by NIS (National Investigation Service) for top secret clearance."

Detective Smyth shot back, "Have you ever been read your rights before?"

The Colonel said, "No."

After reading Williams his rights, Smyth talked about four of the crimes that had been linked, two sexual assaults that happened in Tweed, the murder of Corporal Marie-France Comeau, and the disappearance of Jessica Lloyd.

Smyth then explained the reasons why police had focused on Williams, which included his working relationship with Comeau and him living so closely to both victims. Smyth then asked, "What would you be willing to give me today to help me move past you in this investigation?"

"What do you need?" Williams responded.

"Well, would you want to supply things like fingerprints, blood samples, things like that?"

"Sure," Williams responded.

"Okay, footwear impressions?" Smyth continued.

"Yeah," Williams answered, but now he moved his head facing downwards. They then took a break so that officers could take the samples from Williams.

After that was completed and Smyth came back into

the interrogation room, he noticed Williams was no longer chewing his gum and now had his arms folded, a known defensive body language. He then looked at Smyth and said quite firmly,

---

"Can I assume you're going to be discreet? Because you know this would have a very significant impact on the base if they thought I did this."

After several more hours of talking, Smyth finally decided to drop a bomb on Williams. "Okay, would it surprise you to know that when the CSI officers were looking around her property that they identified a set of tire tracks, along the north tree line? Tire tracks are a major source of evidence for us."

Williams responded, "Sure."

"Shortly after this investigation started, they identified those tires as the same tires on your Pathfinder," Smyth finished.

"Really?" Williams answered seemingly surprised. But now Smyth was about to drop another bomb on Williams.

"All right, this is the footwear impression of the person who approached Jessica Lloyd's house on the evening of the twenty-eighth of January. Okay, this is a photocopy of the boot that you took off your foot just a little while ago, and these are identical, okay?" Smyth then got really stern and finished his theory with, "Your vehicle drove up the side of Jessica Lloyd's house, your boots walked to the back of Jessica Lloyd's house, on the evening of the twenty-eighth and twenty-ninth of January."

The Colonel leaned forward staring at the photo.

"Okay, you want discretion, we need to have some honesty, okay? Because this is getting out of control really fast, Russell, really fast."

Williams sat back in his seat and responded with a "Hmm." After a thirty-second pause he said, "I don't know what to say."

"Well, you need to explain it," Smyth quickly snapped back. "What are you going to do?"

Williams looked up and responded quietly "What's the option?"

Detective Smyth looked at Williams directly into his eyes and said, "Well, I don't think you want the cold-blooded psychopath option. I might be wrong, because I've met guys who actually kind of enjoyed the notoriety."

Williams sighed still with his arms crossed.

Smyth continued, "Is Jessica somewhere we can find her easily?"

After another pause, Williams exhaled deeply. He said, "It's hard to believe this is happening."

Smyth continued, "So, where is she?"

After another twenty-second pause, Williams responded. "Got a map?"

The interview continued for several hours after that, and at one point Williams was formally arrested for the murders of both Marie-France Comeau and Jessica Lloyd, as well as two sexual assaults against Laurie Massicotte and a still undisclosed woman.

Sergeant Smyth then provided Williams with a pad of paper and a pen with a suggestion that he write some letters of apology to his victims. This was not merely for the apologies to the families of the victims; this was also a police tactic to help prevent a claim of false confession by the charged. At first Smyth left the room and gave Williams about a half of an hour, but when he returned Williams had written nothing. So Smyth pressed him again and told him that this was his last chance, then left the room again. When the officer returned, Williams had written a total of eight letters.

LETTER ONE

To Mary Harriman (Williams' wife)

> "I love you, sweet (unreadable). I am so very sorry for having hurt you like this. I know you'll take good care of sweet Rosie (their cat) I love you, Russ"

LETTER TWO

To Roxanne Lloyd (mother of murder victim Jessica Lloyd

> "Mrs. Lloyd, you won't believe me, I know, but I am sorry for having taken your daughter from you. Jessica was a beautiful, gentle young woman, as you know. I know she loved you very much, she told me so, again and again. I can tell you that she did not suspect that the end was coming, Jessica was happy because she believed that she was

coming home. I know you have already had a lot of pain in your life. I am sorry to have caused you so much more."

LETTER THREE

Another draft To Mrs. Lloyd

"I know you won't believe me but I am sorry for having taken your daughter from you. Jessica was a beautiful, gentle young woman. I know she loved you very much. though I forced her to have sex."

Note: (He then scribbled through the lines and stopped writing that letter.)

LETTER FOUR

Another draft to Mrs. Lloyd

"Mrs. Lloyd, you won't believe me, I know, but I am sorry for having taken your daughter from you. Jessica was a beautiful, gentle young woman. I know she loved you very much because she told me again and again. the moment she died she was quite happy, because she believed that I was going to let her go she did not know what was coming."

Again, he scribbled through this letter and stopped writing.

LETTER FIVE

To the undisclosed sexual assault victim

"I apologize for having traumatized you the way [I] did. no doubt you'll sleep a bit easier now that I've been caught."

LETTER SIX

To Laurie Massicotte (second sexual assault victim)

"Laurie, I am sorry for having hurt you the way I did. I really hope that the discussion we had has helped you turn your life around a bit. You seem like a bright woman, who could do much better for herself. I do hope [you] find a way to succeed."

LETTER SEVEN

To Ernie Comeau, father of murder victim Marie-France Comeau

"Mr. Comeau, I am sorry for having taken your daughter, Marie France, from you. I know you won't be able to believe me but it is true. Marie France has been deeply missed by all that knew her."

LETTER EIGHT

To Mr. Comeau, a different draft.

"Mr. Comeau, I am sorry for having taken your daughter from you. I know you won't be able to believe me, but it is the case. I know she has been deeply missed by all that knew her."

Again, he scribbled through the lines he had written and stopped writing.

Early the next morning, Williams led investigators to Jessica Lloyd's body in a secluded area on Cary Road, 13 minutes away from where he lived. Williams was also charged in the death of Corporal Marie-France Comeau, a 37-year-old military flight attendant based at CFB Trenton, who had been found dead inside her home in late November 2009.

Along with the murder charges, Williams was charged with breaking and entering, forcible confinement, and the sexual assault of two other women during two separate home invasions near Tweed, Ontario in September 2009. Per reports, the women had been bound in their homes and the attacker had taken photos of them.

Williams was arraigned and remanded into custody on Monday, February 8, 2010. The Canadian Forces announced that day that an interim commander would soon be appointed to replace him (Dave Cochrane took over 11 days later), and removed his biography from the Department of National Defense website the following day.

Hours after the announcement of Williams's arrest, police services across the country reopened unsolved homicide cases involving young women in areas where Williams, a career military man, had previously been stationed. Per news reports, police began looking at other unsolved cases based on a full statement that Williams gave to police.

Sergeant Smyth was soon granted a warrant, permitting officers to search Williams's cottage on February 11, 2010. Marie Elizabeth, Williams's wife, had been at home when the police arrived to search, with warrant in hand. Harriman was given time to gather her things and leave before they began their search. Detective Sergeant Brian Mason oversaw executing the search warrant. It seemed like an army of police swarmed the residence. There were

12 officers and forensic specialists that arrived in two vans.

During the seven days it took for the police to conduct their search of the cottage, police found red stains consistent with blood on a drawer of the dresser in the master bedroom, on a chair in the living room, and in the bathtub.

The tapes and memory card that contained video footage and pictures of the assaults and rapes on both Marie-France Comeau and Jessica Lloyd were found in the vestibule at the bottom of the piano.

Police also found electrical and duct tape, rope, black zip ties and a duffel bag that was stored in the laundry room cupboard. Inside the duffel bag, there were eight more smaller plastic bags. Here is a listing of what was in each of those bags:

BAG #1

- 93 pairs of women's panties
- 1 slip

BAG #2

- 4 camisoles
- 6 tops
- 13 dresses
- 1 T-shirt

BAG #3

- 2 women's bathing suits
- 2 bikini bottoms
- 8 pairs of panties
- 1 pair of tights
- 18 camisoles
- 1 pair of fishnet stockings
- 1 garter
- 1 garter belt

BAG #4

- 1 nightie
- 1 panty-and-camisole set
- 1 camisole
- 1 pair of panties
- 1 slip

BAG #5

- 51 pairs of panties

BAG #6

- 35 pairs of panties

BAG #7

- 77 pairs of panties
- 3 bathing suit tops
- 2 bras
- 1 bikini bottom
- 2 socks

BAG #8

- 49 bras

In addition to the eight smaller bags of women's garments, the police also found an assortment of sex toys and a 4" X 6" picture of his first assault victim.

It was an interesting thought, how these items were stored in such a place where Williams's wife could so easily have come across them, that she wasn't aware of what he was doing. How would he have possibly explained them to her? Not to mention all the bloodstains found throughout the house. Another point is, why wasn't he trying to hide the items from her? Was he just not worried about what she thought?

The police also found and seized several items from the home:

- Book titled, *LSI guide to lock picking*
- Sony digital camera
- Colonel air force flight suits

- A KRK systems box which contained female underwear and a Ziplock bag full of lubricants
- An APC battery backup box, which contained 4 vibrators, a DVD named *Real Sex Home Videos* and 6 batteries as well as 14 pairs of panties, 34 bras, 2 camisoles and 1 slip
- Computers and associated equipment, which included two external hard drives that had explicit videos and photos of Williams's attacks on both Comeau and Lloyd, as well as a detailed spread sheet of his crimes
- A black skull cap
- Pillowcase with 5 pairs of panties, 1 bra, 2 vibrators, pajama bottoms, a slip and 2 pairs of children's panties
- A green camera bag containing a Sony camera and a pair of women's underwear
- An Epson computer printer box that had 15 pairs of women's panties, 5 bras, a tube of KY jelly, 8 photographs of Jessica Lloyd, Jessica Lloyd's student ID, 4 camisoles and a pair of gray sweatpants

Although it was not revealed to the public, the police also seized photos and videos that showed teenage girls engaged in sexual acts, which was downloaded from the internet onto Williams's home computer. It must be said that they found the same kind of pornography on his work computer located in his office on the military base. To this day, there is still speculation as to why this information was not disclosed. Could this have been an arrangement to protect Williams against fellow prisoners, or just to keep from publicly shaming him? Even more, could this arrangement have been made to protect the military?

What I also found quite interesting is that Williams's wife, Mary Elizabeth, submitted a widely-reported claim against the Ontario Police Department for scratches to her hardwood floors, believed to have happened when the police dragged out the boxes of evidence. She had insisted that the police replace the section of floor that was damaged, not just repair by sanding and coating it.

Police agreed to settle the claim by paying Harriman $3,000 for the damaged floor, as well as another $1,400 to replace a broken lamp, also claimed to have been damaged by the police during their search. Police refused to discuss the payout of the claim, which had really upset the public, as they felt that Williams himself should have been responsible for the damage, rather than the taxpayers.

A week after his arrest, investigators reported that, along with hidden keepsakes and other evidence they had found in his home, they had matched a print from one of the homicide scenes to his boot.

In addition to the four primary incidents, the investigation into Williams included probes into 48 cases of theft of women's underwear dating back to 2006. In the searches of his Ottawa home, police discovered stolen lingerie that was neatly stored, catalogued, and concealed.

Even though Williams was placed on suicide watch at the Quinte Detention Centre in Napanee, Ontario, on April 3, 2010, just one day before Easter Sunday, Williams jammed his cell door lock with cardboard and crumpled foil that he had saved from the juice cups that the prison served for breakfast every morning. He then put a cardboard toilet paper roll, also filled with the same cardboard and foil in it, down his throat.

When the staff heard the gagging noises being made by Williams, they managed to get into the jammed cell door and save his life. On his cell wall, there was a suicide note, written in mustard, which said that his affairs were in order now and that his feelings were too much to bear. After this, the guards used the nickname "Colonel Mustard" anytime they talked about him.

TRIAL OF RUSSELL WILLIAMS

"A criminal trial is never about seeking justice for the victim. If it were, there could be only one verdict: Guilty" - Alan Dershowitz

Mary Elizabeth Harriman was noticeably missing from the hearing following her husband's arrest. She had taken a leave of absence from her job as the associate executive director of the Heart and Stroke Foundation in Ottawa and went into hiding.

There was also a silence amongst her coworkers, as they all refused to speak to the press about anything to do with the case. Williams's mother, who was working at the Sunnybrook Health Science Centre in Toronto, also had not spoken publicly and had avoided all media requests. However, Harvey Williams, Russell Williams's brother, also a family doctor who lived in Bowmanville, a suburb of Toronto, had issued a written statement to the media. He had explained that his brother Russell had been estranged from both him and his mother due to a rift that happened during the separation of their mother from their stepfather.

Harvey also explained that he and his mother had reached out to Russell just over two years earlier, but they had only maintained minimal contact since that time. In fact, Harvey and their mother had showed up to Russell's command ceremony several months earlier, only to be seated in the second row, behind Williams's wife and his stepfather.

It was less than 24 hours after Williams had appeared in court that the base he had formally commanded had a parade for his replacement, Colonel David Cochrane, who had been promoted to the rank of Lieutenant Colonel. Cochrane promised to turn the page and soldier on without looking back. It certainly would be a challenge that would put the base to the test.

On October 18, 2010, Williams pleaded guilty to all charges. On the first day of Williams' trial and guilty plea, details emerged of other sexual assaults he had committed, including that of a new mother who was wakened with a blow to the head while she and her baby were asleep in her house. The first day of trial revealed that Williams also had pedophiliac tendencies, stealing underwear of girls as young as nine years old. He made 82 fetish-related home invasions and attempted break-ins between September 2007 and November 2009.

Williams had progressed from break-ins to sexual assaults with no penetration to rape and murder. He had kept detailed track of police reports of the crimes he was committing, logged his crimes, kept photos and videos, and had even left notes and messages for his victims. In a break-in into the bedroom of a 12-year-old girl, he left a message on her computer saying: "Merci" (Thank you, in French).

He had taken thousands of pictures of his crimes and had kept the photos on his computer. Crown Attorney Robert Morrison presented numerous pictures of Williams dressed in the various pieces of underwear and bras he had stolen, frequently masturbating while lying on the beds of his victims.

Williams entered the courtroom wearing a dark grey suit and quietly pleaded,

---

"Guilty, Your Honor."

The crown attorney Lee Burgess then told the court,

"In relation to each of the murders of Comeau and Lloyd, his crimes have been deliberate, both during committing the sexual assault and while confining the victims."

Jessica Lloyd's mother, Roxanne, was seated in the courtroom holding a large framed picture of her daughter. Also in the courtroom was Laurie Massicotte, Williams's second sexual assault victim, and about 40 victims and family members.

An agreed statement of facts was read out in court following a timeline and escalation of Williams's crimes.

Crown prosecutor Robert Morrison drew attention to Williams's dangerous escalation of repeat break-ins. Morrison said,

> "Williams's repeated sexually obsessive behavior dates to 2007 and 2008, long before he escalated to actual sexual assaults on women, or to the eventual murders of Comeau and Lloyd. In some of the photos, Williams is in girls' lingerie, wearing parts of his Canadian military uniform."

Many of the victim's families had left the courtroom once Williams pleaded guilty. People in the public gallery were shedding tears and shaking their heads. Even seasoned reporters were showing signs of anxiety during the ongoing images that were being displayed.

Speaking to reporters outside the court room was Andy Lloyd, brother of Williams's second murder victim, Jessica Lloyd.

> "I have plenty of friends with teenage daughters, and it's terrible. Nobody likes to hear something like that. Sitting here and hearing stuff that doesn't even involve my sister makes me angry as a Canadian, as a regular human being makes me angry."

Some of the photos presented on the first day of his

trial were published in several newspapers. As some newspapers explained, although troubling, the photos were published because they capture the essence of the crimes of Williams and show the true nature of his crimes. Among the news media that published some of the released photographs were *The Montreal Gazette* and *The Toronto Star*.

On October 22, 2010, Ontario Superior Court Justice Robert F. Scott sentenced Williams to two concurrent terms of life in prison with no chance of parole for 25 years.

The Canadian Forces stripped Williams of his rank and medals and later dishonorably discharged him. At a news conference the afternoon of the plea by Williams, the Department of Defense announced that it would strip Williams's rank, military decorations and honors as quickly as possible. He will not be able to call himself a retired colonel and will simply be a civilian. Before his discharge, he was visited and examined by a military doctor in Kingston Penitentiary, as all outgoing military personnel must undergo a medical examination. Williams's uniform was burned and his medals were later cut into pieces, his commission scroll (a document confirming his status as a serving officer) was shredded, and his Pathfinder was crushed and scrapped.

Williams currently collects a $60,000 annual military pension.

In May 2010, he and his wife also split their real estate holdings, leaving Williams the sole owner of their cottage in Tweed and his wife the sole owner of their Ottawa townhouse.

Williams refused to pay $8,000 in victim surcharge fines, resulting in action being taken against him by a collection agency.

Williams was initially incarcerated at Kingston Penitentiary in the prison's segregation unit. After the prison began the process of closing, he was moved to a maximum-security prison in Port-Cartier, Quebec, on May 10, 2012.

WHO ARE THE PEOPLE IN YOUR NEIGHBORHOOD?

"I want you to be concerned about your next-door neighbor. Do you know your next-door neighbor?"
- Mother Teresa

Orleans, Ontario is known as a quiet family community outside of Canada's capital city of Ottawa, Ontario with a population of about 107,000. It's known for being the home of Elizabeth Manley, who became the 1988 Silver Medalist in Figure Skating at the Calgary Olympic games, and is the home to many of the military and their families, as the National Defense Headquarters in located in Ottawa. Among the residents in Orleans were Russell Williams and his wife, Mary Elizabeth Harriman, who bought a corner lot home on 545 Wilkie Drive, a quiet street for 13 years.

Most nights there was a small gathering of neighbors on Wilkie Drive, usually on the front patio of the Gagne's house. Bob and Terry would welcome Shirley Fraser, George and Shirley White, as well as their newest neighbors, the Williamses. They would often have coffee and talk about local events and gossip.

Quite often they found themselves sitting and watched Russell go on his evening jog, and quite often would tease him. George White remembers Russell coming back from his run and saying to him "Where did you go today, Kanata?" Little did they know what Williams was up to while he was out on his jog, that he was looking for new victims. He would gather as much information as he could so that he could return to their residence and perform one of his many break-ins or perhaps more.

Both Harriman and Williams would cross the street and spend time with their neighbors. Neither would drink coffee, but they would stand and talk. "She was much more talkative, she was more open than he was," remembers Terry Gagne.

"He would look at you every occasionally, but he almost always stared into the ground."

Neither Harriman or Williams discussed much about their private lives during their visits. Shirley White remembers Harriman. "She would discuss her work, her cat, and about golf, but always be very professional." The couple were also known for devoting a lot of time on their cat, Curio. They had no children and often treated Curio as their baby, leaving the blinds open when they were both away. Russ would even have the cat on his shoulder quite often when he came to visit the neighbors for coffee, remembers George Fraser, who fed the cat when they were both away.

Around their home in Orleans, Russ was always seen carrying Mary's luggage in the house for her; he would always hold the doors open for her and was considered very polite.

Harriman and Williams would spend long periods of time apart, as their jobs were very demanding and required them to do quite a large amount of travelling. Then in 2004, they purchased a $178,000 cottage located in Tweed, Ontario, located just over a two hours' drive from their home in Orleans. It was a much smaller community of about 6,000 people, in a mainly rural setting. This was to alleviate the three-hour commute for Russell five days a week when he had to drive to the base to work every Monday through Friday.

Their Tweed neighbor, Larry Jones, says Harriman liked to read paperback novels in a lounge chair. Jones said he would have a glass of wine or beer with the couple every occasionally, and said,

---

"Russ was very polite and formal with his wife in public, always asking her if he could bring her a glass of wine or something. He would also always call her by her first names Mary Elizabeth."

One thing Jones also remembered was that Mary would be in Ottawa most of the time as she worked there, but the Colonel would be there most of the time alone.

> "He was kind of a loner because he never really had any friends there to speak of. Maybe twice a year he'd have some friends there."

One of Williams's visitors at their Cosy Cove Lane cottage in Tweed was Jeff Farquhar, his longtime friend since 1982 when they were roommates in college. "I remember being there when he had first bought it. I think the deal was just barely done and he called me to come out and look, and then gave me a tour," Jeff said.

Both seemed to be enjoying successful careers and continued to advance. Harriman was just promoted as a senior executive for the Heart and Stroke Foundation of Canada. Russell had just advanced to commander of CFB Trenton, the country's largest Air Force base. Shirley Fraser remembers some of the neighbors that had been invited to Russell's promotion ceremony. "Mary Elizabeth seemed thrilled to pieces when the boys had agreed to go down and attend her husband being promoted up in the ranks."

So just a few months later, many on the street were surprised when a "For Sale" sign went up in the couple's front yard. It seems that neither Harriman or Williams had told any of them about their plans. "We were quite shocked when we saw the sign go up," says White "We thought, "Oh, no, they were such great neighbors. What will happen? Who will move in?"

The couple had bought a new high-end townhome in a trendy part of town, on Edison Avenue, Ottawa. Soon afterwards, they said their goodbyes to their neighbors of thirteen years and moved.

Less than two months later, news of Williams's arrest hit the Wilkie Street neighborhood. "A few of us close friends went through three stages," says White "The first stage when the blast of the news came out, we said, can't be, can't be, they've made a mistake, it can't be our Russ."

Then as more details emerged, the group began to think that Williams was guilty, even though they still didn't believe it. White said,

> "Yes, he's guilty. We feel we've been betrayed by the friendship, but anyways life goes on."

George White, a retired Air Force technician, wrote letters to both Williams and Harriman after the news broke about Williams's arrest. To Williams he wrote expressing his regret that the Colonel's life had gone so wrong. To Harriman he wrote that he supported her unconditionally. But neither of them have written back to him.

Shirley Fraser believes that Harriman was victimized by her husband and said,

> "My biggest prayer is that she will be able to get through this. I can't imagine what she's going through."

Harriman was not in Belleville to be with her husband

during his interrogation. In fact, ever since her husband's arrest, she has completely avoided the public spotlight that came with the case. Yet she remains the focus of several lawsuits, being accused of knowing about Williams's sexual assaults and other criminal behavior.

Both court documents and Williams's own recorded confession suggest that Harriman had no idea of her husband's secret life and, in fact, really believed that Russell was a very good person with a fine moral compass. Harriman wrote in the civil suit affidavit.

> "On or about February 8, 2010, I became aware of criminal charges against my husband. The revelation of these charges has been devastating to me."

So far to date, this is all we have heard from her, as she still refuses to speak to any media about her husband.

But there was one neighbor that wasn't so worried about what Williams was going to face in jail. Larry Jones, Williams's Tweed neighbor, had been affected like no other neighbor, as he was a victim as well.

When Williams was arrested, Jones's phone was ringing off the hook from people around the country, either to congratulate him or sympathize with him. In fact, Jones's email inbox was so full that he gave up even trying to answer them.

Per Lloyd, Williams had tried to set him up as the fall guy in his crimes, and it was still one thing that was bothering him. It seemed far too convenient that Russell had placed the body of Jessica Lloyd on the side of the road at the camp where Jones would go hunting. He recalled the conversation that he had with Williams on a previous September day. That day Jones had been dressed in his camouflage gear and loading up his truck with a crossbow and rifle to go hunting. Williams walked over and said, "What's happening today?"

"Oh, I'm just going partridge hunting," Jones responded.

"So, you hunt, do you? There's partridge around here," the colonel asked. Jones thought that was strange as he was sure Williams knew he went hunting a lot and that there was plenty of partridge around the area, but he put it down to an awkward conversation between a city slicker and a country boy.

"There's plenty of partridge out at the camp on East Hungerford Road," Jones told him.

"East Hungerford Road, doesn't ring a bell." Williams questioned him.

"It's out by the golf course, you go up there past Cary Road, and our camp is right there," Jones answered him.

"Oh, really, that's good. Well, good luck with the hunting and we'll see you later," Williams said as he started to walk back to his cottage.

Equally as suspicious, the day before Jessica Lloyd had gone missing, Larry had come home to find his workshop unlocked, even though he remembered locking it the night before, so he quickly looked around inside of the shop. He was worried about all the expensive power tools and equipment that he had stored and bought for his workshop. As he went through everything, he soon realized that nothing major was missing; in fact, the only things gone were an old jacket that was used for the dog to sleep in, and a pair of gloves and his lighter. Who would take the trouble to break into his workshop and take nothing but old used clothing?

Jones now believes that the clothes were stolen either by Williams or by one of the police that had suspected him in the spree of violent crimes. This was the beginning of the nightmare for Larry Jones.

Jones returned home from a partridge hunting trip in October of 2009 to find dozens of police officers going through his home. He was taken in for questioning and, per his statement in a later lawsuit that was filed against the police, officers also interrogated his wife of forty years, asking whether Larry participated in bondage.

He was told that the investigation was related to the break-ins and sexual assaults that were happening around Tweed. But word quickly spread throughout the neighborhood that Jones was a suspect in the case.

One of the sexual assault victims, Laurie Massicotte, told police she couldn't identify her attacker because she had been blindfolded, but thought she might have heard his voice before. She then led the police to believe that the attacker she heard could have been Jones's voice. Massicotte also told police that the attacker was not a tall or big person, between 30 to 40 years old, but Jones was 65 at the time, stood 5'9" and weighed 215 pounds.

Fifteen years earlier, Jones's son, Greg, had worked at Sears with co-worker Warren Lloyd, who just happened to be the father of the second murder victim, Jessica Lloyd. Warren was having problems with his water pump and asked Greg for help with it. Greg had called his father, Larry Jones, and asked him to go over and see if he could fix the pump. Larry drove over to Lloyd's house and fixed the pump without charge. This happens to be the same house that Jessica would later be raped and beaten in. So Larry also knew that his prints were going to be all over that house.

Even when Jones tried to report the break-in of his workshop, OPP Detective Russ Alexander replied, "What do you want me to do about it?" For some reason, Alexander was not letting go of the idea that Jones committed the crimes. In fact, even the day that Williams was being charged and had confessed, Alexander was interviewing witnesses about Jones and the murder of Jessica Lloyd.

Even when Jones's wife, Bonnie, tried to get their belongings that had been seized by the police three months later, she was advised by Detective Alexander that the police were continuing to investigate Larry for the attacks, per the lawsuit documents.

The lawsuit by Jones and his wife was eventually dropped on October 13, 2013. Even though there are still people that no longer speak to him or that look at him in a negative way, Jones looks at it as a valuable learning lesson.

But there was still one thing that had stayed in the back of Jones's mind about his own granddaughters. When all the attacks were happening and they would take the bus out to see their grandfather, if Jones was still out hunting, they would take the bus to Williams's house and wait there for him, as it was considered the safest place for them to wait.

8

WHEN ALL IS SAID AND DONE

"Life is really simple, but we seem to want to make it complicated." - Confucius

Harriman's future once seemed perfectly secure; she and her husband both pulled in six-figure salaries. Their careers were in ascendance. That financial security, however, is now as uncertain as so many of the things that Harriman once took for granted.

The first two multi-million dollar lawsuits, were not only against the convicted murderer Russell Williams, but his wife, Mary Elizabeth, and were filed just four years after his conviction.

Williams's first sexual assault victim, whose name is still withheld from the public, was suing for $2.45 million, and Jessica Lloyd's mother and brother were suing for $4 million. Not only were both parties suing Williams for his brutal and vicious attacks on the victims, but they accused his wife Mary Elizabeth Harriman of participating in a fraudulent property transfer to hide their assets from any lawsuits. Harriman had paid her husband $62,000 in cash and assumed the remaining mortgage on their newly built $700,000 Ottawa home. These lawsuits were settled out of court for an undisclosed amount by Williams himself, and they dismissed the suit against his wife. Despite these settlements, Williams's legal battles were far from over.

Up next was the lawsuit by his second sexual assault victim, Laurie Massicotte. Her claim was for $7 million and, again, it was against both Russell and his wife, Mary Elizabeth Harriman. Massicotte was also charging Harriman as being aware of her husband's home invasions and sexual assaults. She also accused the Ontario Police Department of failing to warn the community about the predator.

Harriman denied any wrongdoing and answered the lawsuit in a court filing saying "I had absolutely no intention of shielding assets" and that "the property deal was initiated to ensure her financial security" She also stated that she was devastated to learn the truth about her husband, and she too was a victim.

Harriman's lawyer, Mary Jane Binks, said that the lawsuit was settled in November of last year, 2016. Binks said,

> "The civil action launched by Laurie Massicotte has now been settled. All parties want their privacy."

Details of the settlement were not disclosed. Massicotte chose to reveal her identity and speak publicly about her ordeal. In her statement of claim, Massicotte said she had been bound and sexually assaulted by Williams in her home in September 2009. She said in the claim that the attack against her left her fearful, humiliated, depressed, suicidal, unable to function in society. It also said she would require extensive therapy.

The Tweed cottage, purchased for $178,000, was transferred to Williams. In 2013, the cottage was sold by Williams to his one-time neighbors and first victims, the Murdochs. They were living right next door to the Colonel, probably sleeping when Williams brought home victim Jessica Lloyd and killed her right in that same cottage. Per their interview with *Macleans* magazine, their motivation was to help the primary victims out by purchasing the property. The money would go to help settle the outstanding lawsuits.

They also want to revitalize the property which has been a long abandoned eyesore. More than anything, they want to ensure Lloyd's devastated family receives the dignity they deserve. "We'll never be able to forget what happened there, even if we rebuild another house on that lot," says Ron. "It's part of the history of that lot. We'll never be able to forget that, and we shouldn't; she lost her life there. But respect will always be given. There will be no cameras in there. There will be no big splash."

You might be asking why the victims and their families were so set on holding Harriman responsible for her husband's crime. There are many things to consider, such as, how it is that Harriman never saw any of the hundreds of pairs of women's panties, bras, dresses and other various pieces of clothing, just lying about the house, in open, unconcealed places, such as the laundry room. How did she not see any of the pictures or films, not only left in many of the bags that were sitting around the house, but also on the MAC computer that she had shared with Williams? On that computer, Williams had put many of the pictures and films of his assaults, home invasions and even ones of the dead victims, all in organized files, where it was easy to access the victim, date and type of crime with one click.

Per *Macleans* magazine, in an interview with Laurie Massicotte, who believed that Mary Elizabeth was aware of her husband's illicit conduct but did not report the crimes to the police. "Massicotte also claims Williams's long-time spouse gained financially from this illicit conduct, by acquiring Williams's assets after he was captured, including half of the couple's new Ottawa home."

Both Laurie Massicotte and Jessica Lloyd's family lawsuits were not only against Russell Williams and his long-time wife, Mary Elizabeth Harriman, but also against the Ontario Police Department. You see, when Williams had assaulted the unnamed victim in mid-September 2009, he left some DNA on her neck. That evidence was processed and uploaded into the RCMP DNA data Bank within two weeks. Later that year, on November 24, was when Williams attacked and killed Marie-France Comeau. Again DNA was taken at the crime scene, but this time it took ten weeks for the police to process and upload it into the same RCMP DNA data bank.

During that ten weeks, Williams had killed again when he tortured, raped, and then murdered Jessica Lloyd. The ten-week time was way over the 30-day target that was suggested by Justice Archie Campbell. A quicker upload would have linked the Comeau murder with the sexual assault in Tweed. We don't know if that would have led the police to investigating a military man, or somebody that was in the living proximity of both victims. I don't think that we could possibly know the answer to that, but it would have significantly advanced the investigation for sure. Andy Lloyd, Jessica's brother, at the time made the statement,

---

> "It doesn't make sense that the DNA results aren't available much faster."

Another strange coincidence that happened with the police was on the night of Jessica Lloyd's murder. While Williams was sitting in his truck, parked on the vacant lot beside her house, waiting for Lloyd to come home, a Belleville police officer spotted his truck. He considered it suspicious and stopped at Jessica's home and knocked on her door. When he received no answer, he left. It was just a few hours later that Jessica arrived home, was assaulted and killed.

EPILOGUE

The One Little Goat theatre company out of Toronto has decided to start running a show this March of 2017 called *Smyth/Williams*. The play is based on the intense interrogation in which Williams ended up confessing to his crimes to then Detective Smyth, per the *Calgary Herald* report on January 23, 2017.

Adam Seelig, the director of the theatre company said,

"I first got the idea for the play in 2010, when Williams's case and confession to Detective Smyth was making all the headlines."

Seelig was amazed at the time by Smyth's ingenuity and chilled by Williams's 'matter-of-fact' manner of confession.

The play will have an all-female group performing as a

direct link to the recent urgency of violence against women, especially against women in the military.

ACKNOWLEDGMENTS

Thank you to my editor, proof-readers, and cover artist for your support!

Evening Sky Publishing Services (book cover), Bettye McKee (editor), Dr. Peter Vronsky (editor), Dr. RJ Parker, VP Publications, Lorrie Suzanne Phillippe, Marlene Fabregas, Darlene Horn, Ron Steed, Robyn MacEachern, Kathi Garcia, Vicky Matson-Carruth, Linda H. Bergeron, James Herington

ABOUT THE AUTHOR

Alan R. Warren is the Host of the Popular True Crime History Radio show '*House of Mystery*' heard in Phoenix on 11:00 a.m. Independent Talk Radio and syndicated throughout the U.S. and Canada. It can also be heard online many different  places from iTunes, YouTube, Tune-in, Stitcher Radio, IHeart Media/Spreaker, Podbay, Podomatic, and at www.alanrwarren.com.

Al has his Doctorate in Religious Studies (DD), Master's Degree (MM) in Music from University of Washington in Seattle, Diploma in Criminology from Douglas College in New Westminster, B.C., Canada, and Recording and Sound Engineering Diploma from the Juno Award Winning Bullfrog Studios in Vancouver, B.C., Canada.

He got his start on Digital Radio for the Z Talk Radio Network and still produces several shows for them.

ALSO BY ALAN R. WARREN

DOOMSDAY CULTS: THE DEVIL'S HOSTAGES

Jim Jones convinced his 1000 followers they would all have to commit suicide since he was going to die. Shoko Asahara convinced his followers to release a weapon of mass destruction, the deadly sarin gas, on a Tokyo subway. The Order of the Solar Temple lured the rich and famous, including Princess Grace of Monaco, and convinced them to die a fiery death now on Earth to be reborn on a better planet called Sirius. Charles Manson convinced his followers to kill, in an attempt to incite an apocalyptic race war.

These are a few of the doomsday cults examined in this book by bestselling author Alan R. Warren. Its focus is on cults whose destructive behavior was due in large part to their apocalyptic beliefs or doomsday movements. It includes details surrounding the massacres and a look into how their members became so brainwashed they committed unimaginable crimes at the command of their leader.

Usually, when we hear about these cults and their massacres, we ask ourselves how it possibly happened. We could also ask ourselves, what then is the difference between a cult and a religion? We once had a small group of people who unquestionably followed a person who believed he was the son of God. Two thousand years later, that following is one of the most recognized religions in the world. This book in no way criticizes believing in God. Rather, it examines how a social movement grows into a full religion and when it does not. And what makes the conventional faiths such as Christianity, Judaism, Islam, and Hinduism stand above groups such as the Branch Davidians or Children of God.

CONFESSIONS OF MURDER: EXPOSING THE FALSE CONVICTIONS CREATED FROM THE MR. BIG STING

It started with a frantic call for help from Sebastian Burns and Atif Rafay, when the two boys arrived home at just after 2 a.m. on July 13, 1994, and found Rafay's family brutally beaten to death in their Bellevue, Washington, home. Who would kill this well-liked family in such a horrific way? Police had no physical evidence and no witnesses; the case was a dead end! It was time to bring in Mr. Big!

Mr. Big is a covert investigation where undercover detectives create a fictitious criminal gang and seduce their suspects into joining them in their criminal activities, and police would soon gain their suspects' confidence and elicit a confession from them. Burns and Rafay would eventually confess on tape to undercover detectives and be convicted of the three murders of Rafay's family.

In the last 25 years, the RCMP (Royal Canadian Mounted Police) have run more than 350 Mr. Big operations on suspects of crimes where there was no evidence found and have had a 95% success rate in prosecution.

It was in July 2014 when the Supreme Court of Canada ruled unanimously that confessions arising from the Mr. Big operations would be considered presumptively inadmissible on another case against Nelson Hart. The Mr. Big Sting in the Hart case was said to have overwhelming inducements, veiled threats of violence, and intimidation and considered an abuse of process by the police.

So now what will happen to the hundreds of other cases that have been tried by this unreliable procedure in which the Mr. Big coerced confession was the only evidence used to convict the suspect? This book will cover the cases that have now been brought back into court on appeals based on the Mr. Big operation, and will explain the outcomes.

REFERENCES

1. Emerson, Dianne: *Psychopaths in our Lives: My Interviews*, Oct. 5, 2016, ISBN-10: 1-517307880, ISBN-13: 978-15170377882, plus a two-hour interview by phone with her about the possible condition of Russel Williams and his family.
2. Appleby, Timothy: *A New Kind of Monster: The Secret Life and Chilling Crimes of Colonel Russell Williams*, August 23, 2011, ISBN-10: 0307359514, ISBN-13:978-0307359513.
3. CBC Fifth Estate: Sept. 24, 2010 Season 36 Episode 1.
4. CBC Fifth Estate: Oct. 22, 2010 Season 36 Episode 5.
5. Pollanen, DR.: Postmortem Exam - Cause of Death, Corporal Marie-France Comeau.
6. Police Transcripts of the videos taken by Russell Williams. The tapes have only been

seen by police, crown prosecutors and defence - cannot be independently evaluated.
7. The Star: *Woman Settles Lawsuit Against Sex Killer Russell Williams and his Wife,* Canadian Press, Oct 12, 2016.
8. Mehta, Diana: *Ontario Woman's Lawsuit Against Russell Williams Settled,* Globe and Mail, Oct. 12, 2016.
9. Rankin, Jim and Contenta, Sandro: *The Secret Life of Colonel Russell Williams Exposed,* Toronto Star, Oct.18, 2010.
10. Friscolanti. Michael: *Serial Killer Russell Williams Has Sold Infamous Cottage,* Macleans, May 22, 2013.
11. Seglins, Steve: *Russell Williams's neighbor Sues After Suspected in Crimes,* CBC News, Nov. 28, 2011.
12. Hendry, Luke: *Lawsuit Against Russell Williams Dropped,* Toronto Sun, Oct. 16, 2013.
13. Gibb, David A.: *Camouflaged Killer: The Shocking Double Life of Canadian Air Force Colonel Russell Williams,* Oct. 4, 2011, Berkely ISBN-10: 0425244393 ISBN-13:978-0425244395.
14. Vronsky, Peter; *Serial Killers: The Method and Madness of Monsters,* Oct. 5, 2004, ISBN-10:0425196402 ISBN-13:978-0425196403.
15. Ottawa Edition: *Accused Killer Colonel Russell Williams and Paul Bernardo,* QMI Agency, Feb. 12, 2010.
16. Tripp, Rob: *Accused Sex Killer Colonel Russell*

Williams Attempts Jailhouse Suicide, Globe and Mail, Apr. 4, 2010.
17. CBC News: *Colonel Russell Williams Pleads Guilty to all 88 Charges*, Oct. 18, 2010.

www.ingramcontent.com/pod-product-compliance
Lightning Source LLC
Chambersburg PA
CBHW072207100526
44589CB00015B/2409